MARJORIE HARRIS
FAVORITE
PERENNIALS

Photographs by **PADDY WALES**

 HarperCollins*PublishersLtd*

First Edition

Canadian Cataloguing in Publication Data

Harris, Marjorie
    Marjorie Harris favorite perennials

ISBN 0-00-255399-6 (bound)
ISBN 0-00-638030-1 (pbk.)

1. Perennials – Canada. 2. Flower gardening – Canada. I. Title. II. Title:
Favorite perennials.

SB434.H37 1994   635.9'32'0971   C94-930695-9

94 95 96 97 98 99 ❖ RRD 10 9 8 7 6 5 4 3 2 1

Printed and bound in Mexico

Design: Andrew Smith
Page layout and composition: Joseph Gisini, Andrew Smith Graphics, Inc.
Editing: Barbara Schon

ACKNOWLEDGEMENTS

Heartfelt thanks go to the people who let Paddy Wales photograph their gardens: University of British Columbia Botanical Gardens; VanDusen Botanical Garden; Capilano Suspension Bridge; Park & Tilford Gardens; Ann Buffam; Francesca Darts; Elizabeth England; Pamela Frost; Thomas Hobbs; Kathy Leishman; Helen and Don Nesbitt; Glen Patterson; Susan Ryley.

    And more thanks go to Barbara Schon for her editing skills, and Maya Mavjee at HarperCollins, who is always on call; to Tom Thomson, Chief Horticulturist at Humber Nurseries, for reading the manuscript; and to Andrew Smith and Joseph Gisini for the book design and Tim Saunders for his good ideas.

    The zones indicated in this book follow the United States Department of Agriculture guide. When there has been conflict over how hardy plants are, I've followed the work done by John J. Sabuco, who seems to have more sense than most people.

COVER: *Paeonia*

Contents

Perennials

It's hard to describe the pure joy of discovering perennials. Like many gardeners, my spring planting used to consist of putting in annuals every year for a garden full of color. But I'd always loved daisies, and when I discovered that these plants were perennial the idea seemed extraordinary—something that would come back every year without any help from me. Years later, that daisy still gives me enormous pleasure. And it's been shared with dozens of people. Not only is perennial gardening less expensive in the long run, it means sharing. A garden filled with cuttings from the gardens of hortbuddies adds a resonance like nothing else.

Perennials won't give the instant hit of color that annuals do, and they may take several years to come into their own. And no matter what you read, you can't be exactly sure how big or wide they will get. Everything in perennial gardening depends on where you are and how you garden.

But none of that should discourage even the wariest gardeners from throwing themselves into perennial gardening with gusto. Perennials return year after year—some for decades, others for only a few years. Many are herbaceous, retreating underground to wait out the winter in dormancy. This makes them tough plants for tough climates because they are right out of winter wind and severe temperatures.

But you ignore adding annuals to the garden at your peril. They add color when bulbs and perennials are out of bloom and keep blooming until frost bumps them off. No garden is complete without the two.

The best thing about perennials is their flexibility. Most can be moved about with impunity from spring to first frost. You can design and rearrange what you want and where you want it. I have plants that haven't rested in years. They are very small. I hate rules, and most gardening doesn't need a lot of them to be successful. One guideline, however, is that if you move a perennial in the middle of a heat wave, it's going to be very, very unhappy.

A garden evolves—that's obvious. Even so, some planning will save time, money and grief in the long run. Once you know where you want to have new borders, live with them for a few days. I've used everything from ropes to hoses to lines of flour or lime to outline how big a new area should be. The point of this exercise is to make sure it's in scale with everything else in your garden—not too big and, most important, not too small. See how it looks from every aspect of your house (including the bathroom window).

*TO IDENTIFY YOUR ZONE, PLEASE SEE THE ZONE CHART ON PAGE 62.

If you start anew in spring, you may want to solarize the dug-up area to clear it of weeds. Cover the disturbed soil with clear plastic held down by bricks and let it sit for a minimum of two weeks. The weed seeds get fried by the sun, but the good things in the soil won't get damaged.

The easiest way to make a new border is to do all the prep in fall. Dig up the soil, add compost, leaves and manure, then let nature do most of the work over the winter. When spring arrives, all this will be well on its way to being humus—the lifeline of soil. Humus is organic material in the process of decay that will feed the soil, ergo the plants, and be light and easy to use. Without humus you've got something akin to rock. Humus helps your soil retain moisture as well as drain properly. This is especially important if the soil is too sandy, has too much clay or is very poor in nutrients.

And God gave us winter as a time for thinking about what to plant in spring. You can always start with seeds, but I think it's much more satisfying, and certainly easier, in the beginning to buy plants.

Chelone obliqua
PHOTOGRAPHED IN THE GARDEN OF: Glen Patterson

Scabiosa caucasica with *Platycodon grandiflorus*
PHOTOGRAPHED IN: University of British Columbia Botanical Gardens

A few caveats here: Stay away from plants and grasses that are too leggy. Alas, you cannot always trust what the labels on nursery plants have to say about color, so if you are buying something expensive look for at least one little blossom that's about to open. Then you'll know the color for certain.

Winter winds and the chill of snow won't harm perennials. But there is another hazard they face—the dreaded freeze-thaw cycle. Plants can be shoved right out of the ground with the action of frost on their roots. Mulching helps keep the root temperature even in both summer and winter. Generally, you take off the mulch around plants in spring so the soil can warm up. Throw it into the compost. After plants are showing new growth, add new mulch. This can be a combination of compost, manure and such material as finely shredded bark (not the big stuff—it looks dreadful) or cocoa bean hulls. These will break down over summer. In autumn, after the first hard frost, add more mulch around the plants to keep them safe over winter.

❧ Don't let mulch touch the stems or crowns of perennials. It might introduce rot or leave a great place for pests to overwinter.

PLANTING

Good planting techniques should never be ignored. Here's how:

Dig a hole that's wider than your plant and deep enough to accommodate all the roots. Water deeply. When the water has drained away, pop in the plant and put it into position, pressing down on the soil hard enough to eliminate all air holes but not so hard that soil becomes compacted. Water deeply once again. When new growth appears, add compost or manure as a top dressing. If it is necessary to add something to the soil, it will be mentioned in the listing in this book. Otherwise, let the plant alone to adjust to the kind of soil you've given it in your garden.

❧ Do your planting when it's cooled down in the evening or on an overcast day. Never let plants sit around getting dried out. Put them in the shade, and soak for several minutes before you start handling them.

❧ Spacing: there is a great temptation to jam stuff in together so you'll have a lush look as quickly as possible. Keep the mature size in mind when you put things in the soil. However, I hate seeing bare ground anywhere, so I don't take my own advice. There are problems with this. Some plants are not going to like a crowded situation, and this may be your most valued or precious plant. The only plants I give lots of space to are peonies—they need a couple of feet all around to be perfectly safe.

PUTTING PLANTS TOGETHER

Now here's where the real fun begins. You can do this on paper if you want, but I like working with the plants themselves. Buying or ordering a lot of plants at once means you can set them in position and move them around for hours before you get down to planting.

Color is always the easiest place to start. You know what colors you like and you can put a number of different species of plants in the same drifts of color. The important principle to observe is not to have only one of everything. One color, one plant plunked into the ground anywhere there's a hole won't make a harmonious whole or reach the goal of renowned garden designer Gertrude Jekyll—"to make beautiful garden pictures."

All through the listings you'll find plant combinations. These are usually ones I've tried in my own garden or observed in others. They are meant only as a jumping-off place.

Time is a major element in putting plants together: when do they bloom and how does the foliage blend? I like to think more about the architecture of a plant than anything else. Getting color echoes (the color from one bloom reflected in another) becomes almost secondary. Contrasts in shape, texture and colors can make a very pleasing arrangement. Verticals add strength to an area of low-growing plants, just as horizontals add an aura of peacefulness. Move from one shape to another gracefully. Dotting plants about creates a dizzying effect. Gardens are supposed to be tranquil places.

It's not necessary to be conventional about the arrangement of your plants: all the biggies at the back, coming down to the little ones. Borders with shrubs and tall and short perennials can move in waves rather than in regiments.

❧ I have two rules about plant choices. One, I'll try anything—including those that aren't supposed to be hardy to my area—again and again and again. Then I give up—in sorrow, knowing this one is definitely not for me. Two, if a plant seems dead I leave it alone for a couple of years—maybe something magical is going on with its root system—and I've often been surprised.

❧ Size: *Big* problem. If a plant is designated as growing to 18 inches (45 cm) when mature and it grows much larger, it may mean your soil is very rich or you live in a sheltered spot. If it won't grow that big, the soil is poorer and so on. The sizes given here are guidelines only, so don't be disappointed.

PROPAGATION

Adding to your stock of perennials is important. Here are a few easy things to do.

❧ Division: Every few years most perennials benefit from being divided up. You'll know when to do this—they collapse in the middle and look awful. Most can be easily divided in halves or thirds by driving a sharp heavy trowel or a small garden spade (the one with a flat bottom edge) through them and carefully extricating the roots, then putting them in prepared holes and watering immediately.

❧ You can also take bits from the outer edges if you absolutely must have another plant.

❧ Plants that creep along the ground usually make new roots where they touch the soil. You can help this along by putting some soil near a node and clamping it in place with a small stone.

❧ Plants such as sempervivens, that grow by rosettes can be cut away from the mother plant and lifted carefully out.

GENERAL PLANT CARE

Deadheading may be one of the most relaxing and satisfying general garden chores. I do it every day simply because it makes me feel good. But the pay-off in most cases is that plants will last longer and perhaps have a second blooming. You will also get to know them better; touching and feeling is as much a part of gardening as digging. A good pair of secateurs, or pruning shears, is the best investment you can make.

❧ Each plant should be examined to see the best place to cut back to, usually to where you can see new growth in an axil—the place between stem and the leaf.

❧ Some plants thrive on being whacked right back in midsummer or after they've first bloomed. These will be mentioned.

❧ If some plants are troubled by fungus and form mildew on the surface, here's a homemade recipe you might want to try. Stir 1 tsp (15 mL) baking soda into 1 pt (500 mL) water and spray the plant from early spring. Make sure vulnerable plants are well watered in early spring and have good air circulation.

My garden isn't terribly floriferous. In fact, many people are disappointed when they see so few things in bloom. Yet I have hundreds of perennials in a small space. I look for softness and delicacy in foliage and I want flowers placed so I can appreciate the blooms and not be overwhelmed by them. I want scent. I want a glow at night. What you want from your perennials may be quite different, and when you give it a little planning will be just as satisfying to you.

Salvia officinalis 'Icterina'
PHOTOGRAPHED IN THE GARDEN OF: Francesca Darts

Artemisia 'Powis Castle'

FAMILY NAME: *Compositae* / ZONE: 5; 3 to 9 depending on the species
PHOTOGRAPHED IN THE GARDEN OF: Pamela Frost

Without a doubt, artemisias are among my favorite plants. Artemisias are available in every region of the country and they share one quality: magnificent silver foliage. Adding these plants to a border, or to a small or large city or country garden, gives cohesiveness to any design.

These powerful plants can also be just as convincing as a statement on their own as specimens. This is certainly true of *A.* 'Powis Castle', which is one of the finest hybrids in this genus. It has a delicate tracery of silver foliage that is like silk feathers. It grows up to 3 feet (1 m) high and 4 feet (1.2 m) wide. Its parents are thought to be *A. arborescens* and *A. absinthium,* both good tough stocks. The foliage is more ethereal looking than in either parent.

It is a woody plant that looks dreadful as winter wears on and it gets more and more soggy looking in the snow. In colder areas it might be killed back, but I've found that with a fair amount of mulching, and patience in spring, it eventually comes back. It is non-flowering, which hardly matters since none of the artemisias are chosen for their little yellow flowers. It thrives in poor soil.

Put this plant where you will brush past it, so you get a whiff of the aromatic foliage. It will grow in zone 4 with protection, will generally get through winters with some die-back in zone 5 and even 6, and in warmer areas won't have any problem at all. It must, however, be mulched in all but the warmest areas.

These plants are in the humongous *Compositae* family, which includes daisies, yarrows and sunflowers and has always been a favorite of the herbalists for both medicine (wormwood to cure worms) and cooking. These herbaceous perennials range from ground-hugging mounds to subshrubs to giants many feet (metres) high. It's a very flexible plant.

When you want to buck up a relentlessly green mass of foliage in the perennial border, try one of these silvery plants. Though I've tried an all-silver border (quite small), it did seem a bit insipid until laced liberally with blue and yellow plants.

Native sagebrushes are valuable landscape plants far too long neglected.

There are adventurous gardeners now who have seen how wonderful they are, especially in dry gardens. Anyone venturing into xeriscaping (gardens designed around drought-tolerant plants) will definitely want to find as many as possible. In prairie landscapes there is no better plant than *A. tridentata*, sagebrush, to act as the outside edge of a garden, to slow down wind and sand and to provide a good backdrop for other plants. With this kind of informal hedging, putting them with silvery trees such as *Elaeagnus angustifolia*, Russian olive, another tough drought-tolerant plant, would give splendid definition to a garden.

I once had six plants of *A. pontica*, Roman wormwood, delivered to my house by mistake. They looked so nice I kept them. Little did I know at the

Artemisia 'Powis Castle'

time just what a spreader this delicate beauty is. The lacy gray leaves and the fresh scent are much to be desired, and I have it as a low hedge around one border. I lop it right back to the ground in midseason and it comes bouncing back very quickly. If you want a plant to fill in empty spaces, this one will perform the task in the worst kind of soil, dead dry spots and partly shady places without a murmur of complaint. So don't listen to those who say it must be avoided.

I currently have ten species of artemisias, as well as several hybrids, and would like to get more if I could find them. To find out more, join societies that have seed exchanges and perhaps you'll find ones not available in the nursery trade.

OTHER SPECIES & CULTIVARS

A. abrotanum, southernwood, is aromatic, reaches 5 feet (1.5m). I started mine from seed and it was fairly easy, but moving it around proved difficult. Southernwood makes a useful aromatic border that can be clipped into shape. Prune in spring.

A. absinthium; the dreaded drug, absinthe, of French poets came from this species. It is also called common wormwood. Of course it's not common at all. It's a tall perennial or subshrub, shrubby at the base; grows 2' – 4' (60 cm – 1.2 m). This European native has become naturalized in North America. It will help keep your garden free of overwintering pests such as slugs. Make a tea with the leaves in fall and pour it around plants that might be attacked; zone 2.

'Lambrook Silver' is the choicest form; lacy foliage; easy to grow; reaches 3 feet (1 m); zone 4.

A. annua, annual artemisia, can be seeded each spring to fill in a spot prettily with scented gray-green erect plants. Will self-seed. Grows very quickly and can take over and be a nuisance if you let it. Grows to 1 foot (30 cm).

A. arborescens is a Mediterranean plant, which means it can take some frost, and though it's supposed to be evergreen it really looks quite ratty during the winter.

A. arbuscula is native to the Rocky Mountains from British Columbia to California. It's a small plant. Good if you have a native garden. Certainly good for a large prairie garden or a xeriscape garden in the west.

A. discolor (syn. *A. michauxiana*) has finely cut silver foliage and I think it is a great plant. Grows from British Columbia to California, east to Alberta, Wyoming and Utah. I've seen it growing naturally in fields. Grows to 18 inches (45 cm).

A. dracunculus, Tarragon; leaves are used in cooking. It is native of all parts of the Northern Hemisphere. Be very careful you don't put in *A. vulgaris* by mistake—it's not a good garden plant, being both coarse, invasive and less flavourfull.

A. lactiflora, white mugwort, can grow to giant proportions—up to 5 feet (1.5 m); a native of China. Unlike other artemisias, it isn't hairy, which might help to identify it.

It has green rather than silver foliage and, more important, showy white flowers. Needs slightly moister soil; sun to partial shade; zone 3.

A. ludoviciana has silver-gray leaves 1½" – 4" (4 cm – 10 cm) long; grows to 3 feet (1 m). Its wonderful foliage mixes in well with other plants. Though it may be considered invasive, it's easy to keep under control. I don't cut it back in fall because it looks lovely all winter. Ideal for a prairie garden or the edge of a woodland.

A. l. var. *albula* 'Silver King' and 'Silver Queen' are the two most famous and attractive hybrids. The latter is much more silvery and reaches to 2½ feet (75 cm). 'Valerie Finnes' is a gorgeous new broader leaf cultivar.

A. pontica, Roman wormwood, grows quickly to its allotted 18 inch (45 cm) width (it grows to 2 feet [60 cm] high) and will spread quickly beyond its proper boundaries (which is anywhere you want it to stay). Ferny pale silver foliage makes it attractive.

A. schmiditiana 'Silver Mound' is a familiar mounding plant 6 inches (15 cm) high with a spread about 1 foot (30 cm); silky texture. From Japan, where it grows by the sea or in the mountains. If it falls apart in the centre in midseason, cut back.
'Nana' is a dwarf form good for the rock garden. Needs full sun; zone 3.

A. stellerana, beach wormwood, will naturally tolerate sea spray. Grows to 2 feet (60 cm) high and 3 feet (90 cm) wide. It's a native of Japan but has naturalized in North America. Likes sandy soil and full sun.
'Silver Brocade', an introduction from the University of British Columbia Botanical Gardens, is a splendid ground-hugging plant; grows to 1 foot (30 cm) high and 2 feet (60 cm) across. Deeply cut lacework, very felted and silver; zone 3.

A. tridentata; the evergreen foliage can reach 12 feet (3.5 m) high. This native of North America is one of the two sagebrushes endemic to North American deserts.

A. vulgaris, mugwort, can be a bad weed; naturalized in eastern North America.

Aster × *frikartii* 'Mönch'

FAMILY NAME: *Compositae* / ZONE: 5; 2 to 8 depending on the variety
PHOTOGRAPHED IN THE GARDEN OF: Pamela Frost

Autumn is my favorite season, and part of the great joy is the appearance of asters. The smells, the rich colors and the variety of sizes and shapes of these marvellous plants mean there is no such thing as too many in any garden.

They have different cultural requirements, so it's important to be aware of what you are putting into the garden. Some will drop all their bottom leaves if they get stressed.

Aster means star in Latin, and that's exactly what the flowers look like. Generally they bloom in August and September, and some continue blooming until frost. The color range is superb—muscular tones of purple, pink, red, blue and white.

The hybrids we know are derived from two natives: *A. novae-angliae*, New England aster or Michaelmas daisy, and *A. novi-belgii*, also called Michaelmas daisy after the feast of St. Michael the Archangel.

A. × *frikartii* is one of autumn's best plants. It blooms for ages from late summer right up to frost and grows 3' – 4' (1 m – 1.2 m). It's more upright and less shrubby than other asters and has big lavender blue flowers with yellow centres. This hybrid is a cross between *A. amellus* (a native of Italy) and *A. thomsonii* (Himalayan). Two selections are relatively easy to find: 'Mönch', an amazing plant that blooms for months, and 'Wonder of Staffa'. In colder areas they might be tender; zone 5.

Asters can be divided into three kinds:
1. Asters for rock gardens, dry gardens and containers: *A.* × *alpellus*, *A. alpinus*, *A. amellus*, *A.* × *frikartii*, *A. spectabilis* and *A. tongolensis* form clumps and need full sun and rich, well-drained soil.
2. Asters for the border: This group grows in marshes, at roadsides and in meadows; needs average soil that's evenly moist. *A. novae-angliae*, New England aster, *A. novi-belgii*, *A. umbellatus* spread rapidly and need dividing regularly to keep them in line. Get rid of any old woody portions.
3. Woodland species: *A. divaricatus* and *A. macrophyllus* accept shade and moist, rich soil.

Aster x *frikartii*

New England asters will lose their lower leaves and look quite sad if you do nothing to them. I usually cut them back by half in June. In fact, pinching any aster back early in the season helps make it stand more upright, be more compact in form and more free-flowering. Of course, it probably means they bloom later, but the wait is worth it.

I am particularly crazy about asters combined with *Coreopsis verticillata* 'Moonbeam', with its fine threadlike foliage and pale lemon flowers. Another good mate for them is the more invasive *Lysimachia clethroides*. And any of the great artemisias, of course. I also have them with chelones, the Turtleheads, whose starchy presence looks good with the more ferny foliage of the asters.

OTHER SPECIES & CULTIVARS

A. alpinus 'Albus', rounded white flowers with yellow eyes; compact; 10 inches (25 cm); can take some shade; blooms June to September.

'Happy End', semi-double lavender flowers; grows to 1 foot (30 cm); zone 4.

A. cordifolius, blue wood, pale lavender flowers; grows to 2½ feet (75 cm).

A. divaricatus, white wood aster, grows to 2 feet (60 cm) with white ray-flowers and yellow disc-flowers on woody stems; will take the shade; zone 4.

A. ericoides, heath aster, white starry flowers with maroon centres; grows to 3 feet (1 m).

'Pink Cloud', pale pink daisy-like flower heads. Attracts bees and butterflies; zone 3.

A. novae-angliae, cultivars of interest: zone 4

'Harrington's Pink' is a highly invasive, absolutely gorgeous 5 foot (1.5 m) clear pink form.

'Alma Potschke', salmon rose flowers; grows to 3 feet (1 m); blooms for at least six weeks.

'Autumn Snow' (syn. 'Herbstschnee'), a German hybrid, large white flowers; grows to 5 feet (1.5 m).

'Hella Lacy' bears the name of the great aster fancier Alan Lacy's wife; purple flowers; grows to 3½ feet (1 m).

A. novi-belgii, cultivars of interest: zone 4

'Climax', blue flowers; grows to 5 feet (1.5 m).
'Fellowship' has pale pink flowers with yellow eyes; grows to 4 feet (1.2 m).
'Professor Anton Kippenberg', blue semi-double flowers; grows to 1 foot (30 cm).
'White Ladies', white with almost orange centres; grows to 6 feet (2 m).
'Crimson Brocade', reddish pink; grows to 3 feet (1 m).

Chelone obliqua

FAMILY NAME: *Scrophulariaceae* / ZONE: 3; to 6 depending on species.
PHOTOGRAPHED IN THE GARDEN OF: Glen Patterson

The perennial border begins to look a bit sad by August. There is a hiatus just after the great flush of June and July and before the wonders of autumn color. It's fun to plant especially for this downtime. Turtleheads are about the best plants I know to bridge the blossom gap until fall.

These curious plants look a bit like the origin of the name, which is from the Greek *kelone*, tortoise. The swollen upper part of the blossom has a head-like form that overlaps the lower part of the bloom, giving it the appearance of a turtle's mouth about to snap. Bees will disappear right inside the bloom to get at the nectar. The opposite leaves are stiff and a dark satiny green.

What is particularly charming about this plant is that as one terminal bloom fades another opens up slightly below it. As the flowers get past their prime, fat seedheads that are just as attractive start to form. Leave the

Chelone obliqua

seedheads alone—they are ornamental as well. On the whole it's a plant that gives good value.

Once included in the genus *Penstemon*, chelones have a resemblance to them. Those with cottages near wetlands may see these plants in the wild. Their range is from Ontario east to Nova Scotia and south to Georgia and Missouri. Check out abandoned sites, roadsides and any place near the edge of water to see these plants in their natural habitat.

C. obliqua, rose turtlehead, is considered the best of the lot. This native of the southern United States grows in swamps. Has leaves 6 inches (15 cm) wide. Flowers are pink with a yellow-bearded lower lip. This is a heavier-flowering species than the others. Very upright; grows to 3 feet (1 m). Prefers moist, acid soil and will grow in sun or partial shade.

'Alba' has white flowers.

I have chelones mixed in with Japanese anemones that bloom later in the season, and *Eupatorium*, Joe-pye weed, a statuesque plant that is also a great flower for drying. Another good autumn perennial is *Physostegia virginiana*, false dragonhead. The pink flowers complement the chelones, and it's about the same size. It is quite unruly in its spread, however. A white form, 'Alba', and a slow-growing 'Variegata', with creamy-edged foliage and pinky lilac flowers, are both good with chelones.

PLANTING & MAINTENANCE TIPS

❧ This plant takes moist, even soggy soils in sun or shade and can be divided easily. The only problem it might develop is mildew. Make sure that it has good air circulation and gets plenty of water, especially in spring. If you do have problems with mildew, start fairly early on to spray it with a mix of 1 tsp (15 mL) baking soda in a pint (500 mL) of water.

OTHER SPECIES & CULTIVARS

C. glabra, white turtlehead, grows to 5 feet (1.5 m) with leaves 6 inches (15 cm) long. Native to Ontario and Newfoundland, south to Georgia in wet places. A vase-shaped plant with white to pale pink tubular flowers with a white-bearded lower lip and dark green opposite leaves; zone 3.

C. lyonii, pink turtlehead, grows to 3 feet (1 m) high. The bright rose pink flowers have a lower lip with a yellow beard. The lush shiny leaves are 4" – 7" (10 cm – 18 cm) long. Native to the southern United States, where it grows in wet soils; does fairly well in sun and shade. The flowers sometimes seem to be right in the leaf joints (axils); zone 3.

Coreopsis *verticillata* 'Moonbeam'

FAMILY NAME: *Compositae* / ZONE: 3 to 5 depending on variety
PHOTOGRAPHED IN THE GARDEN OF: Francesca Darts

Coreopsis verticillata

There are some plants that refresh the soul. Coreopsis, especially *C. verticillata* 'Moonbeam', is one of them. A cloud of the palest yellow daisy-like flowers floats gently in the midst of the perennial border. This clear color accomplishes what few colors—other than white—can do: it harmonizes various colors and offers unity in any disparate situation.

    C. v. 'Moonbeam' has needle-like slender leaves that support the pale flowers in a most bewitching manner. Stems grow 1' – 3' (30 cm – 1 m), though in my experience they check in pretty consistently at 2 feet (60 cm). It's a mounding plant with masses and masses of pale yellow flowers that carry on until autumn frosts if you keep deadheading it. There are many really good

🌿 Likes a light sandy loam with not too much humus added. Leave about 15 inches (45 cm) between plants. Keep deadheading for months of bloom.

🌿 Propagate by division, from seed or from cuttings. Sow seeds of the annual coreopsis in place once soil has warmed up in spring.

🌿 Divide in fall or early spring. Doesn't mind transplanting.

🌿 I've never seen anything munching away on this plant, not even slugs. Mildew may affect it if it's planted too intensively. If it does, just cut back.

🌿 Lashings of compost, and mulch during hot periods, maintain a cool soil.

forms among the threadleaf types. One enchanting combination, I find, is a *C. v.* 'Zagreb' with a pale blue aster near a small arctic willow. They are all about the same size and seem to dance with each other.

There is a superb species called *C. rosea*. It's smaller, the pink is particularly clear, and it is native to the North American east coast. It's terrifically hardy, but grows slowly. Mine has been trapped under ice and floods and has endured famine. It survives. What a plant for an impossible site.

There are 115 to 120 species spread around North America and Africa and they are in the same family as daisies. There are annuals, biennials and perennials. Most have branchless stalks and leafy bracts just below the flower heads. The rays are usually some form of yellow or gold, with the exception of the pink form and occasionally a bicolor.

OTHER SPECIES & CULTIVARS

C. auriculata, native from Virginia to Florida, good for the rock garden; it has bright orange-yellow flower heads 2 inches (5 cm) across; roundish leaves; zone 4.

C. grandiflora; the large orange-yellow blooms are 3 inches (12 cm) across; grows to 3 feet (1 m). 'Early Sunrise', similar to the above, with double flowers.

C. lanceolata, native from Ontario to Florida; there are many hybrids of this species. Yellow daisy-like flowers grow 2½ inches (7 cm) across; reaches 2 feet (60 cm).

'Sunray' has bright yellow flowers in late spring; grows to 18 inches (45 cm).

C. rosea, grows to 2 feet (60 cm); stoloniferous; likes a moist soil. Zone 4.

Annual coreopsis:

C. tinctoria, native from Saskatchewan and Minnesota west to Washington and California; has golden yellow flowers with red centres; grows to 2 feet (60 cm); endures poor soil and drought. Sow in place in spring.

'Nana' has lilac pink florets; dwarf form grows to 8 inches (20 cm).

Euphorbia myrsinites

FAMILY NAME: *Euphorbiaceae* / ZONE: 5; 4 to 6 depending on the species
PHOTOGRAPHED IN THE GARDEN OF: Glen Patterson

Euphorbias are among the most tailored and elegant of all plants—though they do have blooms, it's for their shape, form, texture and color that we grow them. They are the kind of plants that have surfaces so tempting you want to reach out and touch them.

Euphorbia myrsinites

This enormous family comprises more than 1,600 species, from tiny weeds to gigantic trees. Many of them have the look and feel of succulents. It even includes *Euphorbia pulcherrima*, the familiar poinsettia. There are annuals, herbaceous perennials, succulents, desert plants, tropical shrubs and annuals. But the ones I love are the hardy herbaceous species that will grow in most gardens.

The foliage of these plants often has a bluish green cast, which is even more lovely than the bracts (modified leaves) that carry the color rather than the almost inconspicuous flowers. Though a few of them are evergreen and will give some shape to the winter garden, all of them help disguise spring bulbs and continue to shine all summer and look truly splendid in the autumn. There are three types of spurge: those with tap roots from a central woody crown; those with running roots; and those with central crowns.

E. myrsinites, myrtle euphorbia, was labelled "donkey's tail" when I bought my first one. I couldn't resist the gray foliage and its trails of thick, fleshy stems radiating out from the woody base. It needs sun and it must have good drainage. I've found to my chagrin that left in a wet spot this euphorbia will simply fall apart. This is a prostrate plant, with strong gray-green leaves, sulphur yellow bracts and tiny flowers in early spring. The ropy stems flop about looking vaguely exotic, a little bit like eucalyptus. There are dwarf forms that are exquisite in the rock garden.

PLANTING & MAINTENANCE TIPS

❦ These plants must have well-drained soil. If they sit around in a lot of moisture, they will just rot away. To bring out their best autumn color, grow them in full sun. They can tolerate both full sun and part shade in ordinary to poor garden soil. In hot areas they do better in slightly filtered shade. Some are drought tolerant.

❦ Without snow cover, make sure that they are either in protected places or covered with pine boughs to keep the leaves and stem from harm.

❦ If the plant gets leggy in summer, cut it back.

❦ On evergreen euphorbias, cut off the dying bloom stalks.

❦ To propagate, take cuttings from the tip in summer. Divide in fall—cut the roots cleanly. Do this every three years.

❦ Mulch in early spring preferably, with pine bark. This helps keep the clumps from being stripped clean by heavy spring rains and being exposed.

Because of their strong steel blue foliage, they look wonderful with perennials that have a similar bent: *Dianthus* spp., or more brilliant low creepers such as *Phlox subulata* and sedums, which also have fleshy stems.

I've put euphorbias in various situations in the garden. The architectural form of the plants means they won't take a lot of competition so need something low or with simpler foliage as a contrast. The architectural form also makes them particularly good with shrubs and evergreens—next to *Daphne burkwoodii* 'Silver Edge' or *E. amygdaloides*, for instance. Early blooming *E. characias* will complement spring bulbs. Any euphorbia combines very well indeed with artemisias and stachys. Some, such as *E. cyparissias*, make excellent ground covers. Since many of them look absolutely gorgeous in fall, plant them with asters and chrysanthemums for a double hit.

OTHER SPECIES & CULTIVARS

E. amygdaloides tolerates dry shade and is a fast spreader. Erect, branching from the base. Lime green flower heads. The new leaves start out red and evolve to gray; yellow bracts; zone 6.

    var. *robbiae* has dark green glossy leaves; pale green bracts; grows to 2 feet (60 cm).

    var. *rubra* has purple-red foliage.

    'Variegata' has creamy margins and grows easily from cuttings; zone 7.

E. characias is a native of southern Europe. A woody perennial with evergreen blue–gray lanceolate leaves 4 inches (10 cm) long arranged in spirals; yellow-green flowers.

    var. *wulfenii* grows to 6 feet (2 m).

E. corollata, flowering spurge, grows to 3 feet (1 m) and dies right back in winter. Leaves are 1" – 2" (2 cm – 4 cm) long; flower clusters at top of plant have white bracts. Native to eastern North America. Zone 3.

E. cyparissias, European, naturalized in eastern North America. Upright stems; about 1 foot (30 cm) high with feathery leaves. Bracts are red-purple. Zone 4.

E. griffithii 'Fireglow' grows to 3 feet (1 m) with green foliage and orange-red flowers in early summer. Zone 4.

E. lathyris, caper spurge or mole plant, is supposed to discourage these pests from the garden. I have never had moles, so maybe it's true. The erect shape with the dark green-purple tone of the almost perpendicular leaves (2" – 6" [4 cm – 15 cm]) is striking. Grows to 3 feet (1 m). A biennial.

E. marginata, snow-on-the-mountain, is the old-fashioned annual. Both the flowers and the leaves have broad white margins. It can be sown in place in early May. Very decorative in a vegetable garden.

E. polychroma (syn. *E. epithymoides*) is considered choice. A dazzling plant in early spring. It is probably the best spurge for Northern gardens. Very showy yellow flowers in early May. Good foliage that takes on Autumn tints. Zone 4.

MEADOW SWEET, DROPWORT

Filipendula ulmaria 'Aurea'

FAMILY NAME: *Rosaceae* / ZONE: 3
PHOTOGRAPHED IN THE GARDEN OF: Elizabeth England

Many years ago when a *Filipendula* made its first appearance, I thought of it as the magic mystery plant. It was given to me unlabelled, and when it grew it seemed to rise like a foamy tide above the other plants and in death scattered its white petals like a soft fall of snow. Magic, indeed.

Filipendulas are not to be taken on lightly in a small garden. Many are large plants in every sense of the word—in size as well as in presence. They work best with other imposing plants or small shrubs as long as they are in scale with each other.

The rather ragged-edged maple-type leaves are strong elements in any border design and the great plumes of flowers range from pale ecru to pure

Filipendula ulmaria 'Aurea'

❧ Most of these plants like a fairly moist soil. Divide every few years and keep mulched during the winter.

❧ Spider mites will infect plants if they are too dry. Cut any infestations right down to the ground.

white to the richest of pinks. They are damp-loving plants perfect for siting beside streams or ponds or in any wet situations. Otherwise, combine them with plants equally striking in size and shape.

F. ulmaria, Queen-of-the-meadow, is a European native that has become naturalized in the wetlands of North America. Imposing with its large, veined basal leaves with rather jagged edges; golden green with white hairs underneath. Fragrant white plumes of flowers in midsummer aren't up to much, but that doesn't matter.

'Aurea', which is shown here, is a magnificent plant, which grows to 3 feet (1 m) with a width of 1 foot (30 cm). This yellow form is a glorious shade of pale gold that turns a golden green as the season progresses—a marvellous plant for a drift of yellow. To keep it looking fresh, chop back in the middle of summer to get a fresh flush for fall.

OTHER SPECIES & CULTIVARS

F. palmata, Siberian meadow-sweet, for moist areas; grows to 4 feet (1.2 m); forms clumps, with five-lobed palmate (that is, palm-like) leaves, white hairs beneath. Pale pink plumes. Zone 2.

'Nana' is a dwarf variety that may bloom up to September, with the right moist soil conditions. Zone 2.

F. purpurea is a tender form from Japan; fragrant with deep pink flowers on red stems. Grows to 4 feet (1.2 m). Full sun and moist soil. Zone 6.

F. rubra 'Venusta', Queen-of-the-prairie, has deep rose or purplish red flowers. Grows to 8 feet (2.5 m) with a spread of 4 feet (1.2 m); fairly rampant, almost massive in the right situation, in either sun or shade. Don't go near this one unless you have a ton of space. Native American hardy to zone 3.

F. ulmaria 'Flore Plena' has white double flowers and finely cut leaves. Grows to 4 feet (1.2 m). Needs moist soil. Prone to mildew. Zone 3.

F. vulgaris (syn. *F. hexapetala*), dropwort, is a European native and loves dry grassland in its native habitat. Finely divided foliage; feathery white flowers. Zone 3.

'Flore Plena' has double flowers, more finely cut leaves; smaller at 1 foot (30 cm). Can take slightly drier soil. Zone 3.

Gaura lindheimeri

FAMILY NAME: *Onagraceae* / ZONE: 5
PHOTOGRAPHED IN THE GARDEN OF: Glen Patterson

Gaura lindheimeri

Poor gauras. First they were greeted as just the ticket to fill out the summer garden. Then they were dumped on by grumpy garden writers saying it's just a fad plant and not up to much. I don't care. I like gauras because they have delicate butterfly-like blooms at the end of willowy almost wire-thin stems. Even in horticulture there are styles and fads that come and go without explanation. But it's fitting to note that the word *gauros* means superb in Greek. Though I would not go that far in describing these plants, the flowers have an ethereal quality to them in a pink to white mix on long, slender gray-green stalks. The flowers are described in

Hortus as being spicate racemes or panicles, which doesn't seem to do justice to these wispy phantoms. There are 18 species, both perennial and annual, native to North and South America. It is a member of the evening primrose family.

G. lindheimeri, white gaura, seems to go on and on, blooming from June until October. Flowers start out white and turn more and more pink as they mature, then drop off without going all brown. The lance-shaped leaves are 3 inches (7.5 cm) long, have no stalks and are mainly at the base of the plant. Grows usually to 4 feet (1.2 m), but has been known to reach 5 feet (1.5 m), with a spread of 2' – 3' (60 cm – 1 m). It's a native of Texas and Louisiana, where it grows in prairie settings.

This one forms long tap roots, which makes it hard to divide. But I'm not sure you'd want to do this anyway. One or maybe two of them are enough for any garden. If it gets too floppy, clip it back to about a foot (30 cm). Propagate by division or from seed. It is unbelievably tolerant of dry heat.

Combine it with *Achillea* 'Snow Taler', a ferny-leaved yarrow with pure white flowers. The two are quite magical together. Others to consider: *Liatris spicata*, blazing star; *Sedum spectabile* 'Autumn Joy'; and it will cover up the bottom stretches of cosmos and make it more at home in the border.

PLANTING & MAINTENANCE TIPS

❧ Most soils seem to suit this plant but it doesn't do as well in rich clay or sandy soil. Tolerates high humidity and a certain amount of drought. Needs sun and a well-drained location. Puts up with all sorts of abuse.

❧ Cut off the spikes to keep it in shape in the border. If you cut it right back in midsummer, it will become fuller, but you don't have to worry about deadheading.

❧ This is not a difficult plant to grow from seed and will flower in its first year. You can even take cuttings while the plant is in bloom.

❧ In zones 5 and 6 it will need a thick mulch.

OTHER SPECIES & CULTIVARS

G. coccinea, scarlet gaura, is native to dry prairies from Alberta to Mexico; has gray stems and leaves. Flowers open white to pink and get increasingly redder in maturity, especially in hot dry sites. The scented blooms open in the evening. Grows to 18 inches (45 cm). Moths love this plant. Zone 3.

Geranium cinereum 'Ballerina'

FAMILY NAME: *Geraniaceae* / ZONE: 5; from 4 depending on the species
PHOTOGRAPHED IN THE GARDEN OF: Susan Ryley

There isn't a geranium I don't like. I don't mean the exotic tender plants we normally call geraniums (those are actually pelargoniums); I'm referring to cranesbills, or hardy geraniums. There are many that will grow in the shade, but the ones listed here love the sun.

Geranium cinereum 'Ballerina', shown on the left side of the picture, is a splendid plant for the front of the border. It grows in an 8 inch (20 cm) mound. The delicate flowers are typical of geraniums, with five simply shaped petals. In this case they are veined in a deeper shade of pink and give the flower an opaque look, as though you are seeing veins through alabaster skin. The deep green leaves set them off dramatically.

Putting geraniums in the garden means being just a bit careful. Some of the more readily obtained forms are magenta with a lot of blue. Not always easy to combine with other colors.

One combination I like is *G. endressii* with *Fragaria* 'Pink Panda' (strawberry), and *Artemisia pontica*. These three somewhat invasive plants can ramp around each other without any problems and they look glorious in their pink, green and gray beauty. They can be cut back in midseason to keep them under control and can be easily divided to confine them.

Another glorious plant that should have a home in every garden is *Dianthus* x *allwoodii*, with its steel gray foliage. It is superb with geraniums, as are almost all of the artemisias.

PLANTING & MAINTENANCE TIPS

❧ Geraniums, happily, don't need especially good soil, but they do like regular watering. I haven't found any particular pests that attack this plant. They make good cover-ups because weeds just can't penetrate the thick base. Most will flower for well over a month and will repeat with cutting back. To add to your stock, take pieces from the edges of the plant rather than pulling the whole thing up and dividing.

Geranium 'Russell Prichard' to the right and *G. c.* 'Ballerina' to the left
with *Stipa gigantea* and *Acanthus mollis*

Many geraniums look good humped up against other plants to keep them from flopping about all over the place.

OTHER SPECIES & CULTIVARS

All the following plants prefer sunny locations. If they tolerate some shade, that is indicated.

G. x *cantabrigiense* 'Biokovo' is a wonderful ground cover from the former Yugoslavia, with evergreen foliage and white flowers. It also works in semi-shade. Grows on 6" – 8" (15 cm – 20 cm) stems.

G. dalmaticum is excellent for the rock garden or as an edger; has pink flowers and glossy leaves with good fall color. Grows 6 inches (15 cm).

G. himalayense (syn. *G. grandiflorum*) is one of the parents, along with *G. pratense*, of the great hybrid 'Johnson's Blue'. A spreading mat that does well in mountain locations; deep blue flowers with overlapping petals May to July. Will tolerate drought and some shade; the foliage turns a wonderful color in fall.

'Gravetye' has large blue flowers.

'Birch Double' is smaller and more purple than blue.

G. maculatum, native of eastern North America to Manitoba, grows in wet places; has narrow leaves and many lilac pink flowers from April to July. Needs good soil—better than other geraniums listed. Grows to 2 feet (60 cm).

G. x *magnificum* has violet flowers and dark green foliage; doesn't develop seeds, since it is sterile. Grows to 2 feet (60 cm).

G. pratense, meadow cranesbill, native of Europe; upright, deeply divided leaves with saucer-like flowers that bloom June to September. Watch that it doesn't self-seed all over.

'Mrs. Kendall Clarke' is blue; grows to 2 feet (60 cm).

G. renardii, native to the Caucasus Mountains; blooms June to July, white flowers with purple veins. Puckered leaves have deep clefts, slightly scalloped edges and are almost sage green. Grows to 10 inches (25 cm).

G. sanguineum, bloody cranesbill, native to Europe and Asia; this one will almost grow on rock, and can be planted by the sea. The flowers are magenta and need cutting back after the first flowering to look good; blooms from April to August; deeply divided dark green leaves with 5 or 7 lobes; each lobe is further divided making a lovely foliage. The flowers are 1 – 1.5" (2.5 – 4.2 cm) wide. Spreads about 1 foot (30 cm).

'Album' is the white form and just as adaptable as the above, if not more so. Combines beautifully with almost everything. Protect from glaring sun in hot areas. Grows to 18 inches (45 cm).

var. *striatum* (syn. *G. lancaster*) 'Lancastriense' has pale pink blossoms streaked with red, 10 inches (25 cm) which bloom in June. Will also repeat if deadheaded. Plant with dianthus and santolina.

G. wallichianum is superb in rock gardens or as an edger. Needs well-drained soil; lavender blue flowers with white centres.

'Buxton's Blue', clear blue with white centres.

Heuchera
micrantha var. *diversifolia* 'Palace Purple'

FAMILY NAME: *Saxifragaceae* / ZONE: 3 and 4
PHOTOGRAPHED IN: University of British Columbia Botanical Gardens

Coral bells are lovely old-fashioned plants essential as part of a traditional garden. 'Palace Purple', one of the finer hybrids, is a wonderfully dramatic plant with extraordinary bronze-purple leaves. The value of heucheras lies in their toughness and longevity. As well, they make fantastic cut flowers.

Heuchera sanguinea is the traditional coral bells familiar to most gardeners. It is parent to the amazing variety of hybrids found in the nursery trade now. There are approximately 70 species, all of them native to North America and many from the Rocky Mountains.

Delicate flowers hang daintily from the top of wiry stems and nod over the low-growing mass of foliage. The foliage is lush, starting out in spring in almost copper tones with the texture of satin. The lobed or toothed leaves slowly turn vermillion in the fall.

H. micrantha 'Palace Purple' is a hybrid from the famous Kew Gardens in England. It's a form of *H. micrantha* var. *diversifolia*. They are striking at

Heuchera micrantha var. *diversifolia* 'Palace Purple'

PLANTING & MAINTENANCE TIPS

❧ Heucheras like soil to which compost, leaf mold or humus has been added. Make sure the drainage is good. They are best in the sun, especially the more brilliantly colored leaf forms, but will cope with part of the day in the shade. Keep deadheaded and they'll keep on blooming.

❧ Plant in spring or early fall and set the crown about 1 inch (2.5 cm) below the surface. If you are using them in drifts or as ground covers, plant 1 foot (30 cm) apart.

❧ Make sure the plants are watered in dry weather. Mulch, since they are shallow rooted and subject to freeze-thaw heaving. (See Introduction.)

❧ Divide every three to five years or whenever you think there are fewer blooms on shorter stalks; or when the crowns get too woody—they tend to die off.

❧ Adding compost around the plant encourages new fibrous roots.

the front of a border or as an edger. The maple-shaped leaves soften just about any form of stone or brick that demarcates a border. They look wonderful in drifts of three to five plants, with shrubby plants such as *Artemisia* 'Powis Castle'. It's magic to see the low-growing purple leaves and the tiny flowers rubbing up against the silver threads of the artemisia. Or with *Alchemilla mollis*, Lady's-mantle, whose leaves are the perfect complement.

Most heucheras take about three years to get well established, so don't be impatient. They aren't fussy if you follow good planting tips.

OTHER SPECIES & CULTIVARS

H. americana 'Chocolate Ruffles', leaves are chocolate on top and burgundy on bottom with white bells on purple stems.

'Emerald Veil' has light green flower spikes with dark green leaves 5 inches (15 cm) wide. 'Persian Carpet' has purple stems and green and purple flowers.

H. x *brizoides* is a hybrid of *H. sanguinea* and *H. micrantha*. Will take some shade. Grows to 2½ feet (75 cm). There are dozens of hybrids.

'Pluie de Feu' has scarlet flowers. 'White Cloud' has white flowers.

H. cylindrica 'Green Ivory' is a startling form with blunt lobes and greenish flowers. Grows to 3 feet (1 m), with a spread of 1 foot (30 cm).

H. x *heucherella* is a cross between *Tiarella* and *Heuchera* and a fine plant in itself. The one I'm most familiar with is x *h. tiarelloides* 'Bridget Bloom', with tiarella-type foliage; slow grower with pink flowers. There is also x *h. tiarelloides* with pale pink flowers.

H. sanguinea, coral bells; the red-flowered parent of most of the hybrids. A tough old-fashioned plant; grows to 1½ feet (45 cm); zone 3.

Iris ensata

FAMILY NAME: *Iridaceae* / ZONE: 3
PHOTOGRAPHED IN THE GARDEN OF: Kathy Leishman

Iris ensata (syn. *I. kaempferi*)

Iris collectors are just as crazed, perhaps slightly more so, as any other plant collectors. Where there is soil there are irises, from the edge of the sea to alpine meadows. They grow on bulbs, rhizomes and rhizomatous roots. They can be grassy or fan-shaped, but usually they are divided into bulbous and non-bulbous (rhizomatous) species.

Iris ensata (syn. *I. kaempferi*)

My preference is for non-bearded irises; maybe it's having a small garden that just won't accommodate the kind of space some of the big prima donna bearded types demand. I just have too many plants in the garden for this luxury. Bearded rhizomes need lots of sun for blooming the following year, and I can't guarantee that, either.

Naturally, there are exceptions to every rule, and in this case it's *I. pallida*, especially the variegated form. *I. pallida* 'Variegata' is a stunner—gray leaves with creamy margins. The pale blue flowers are lovely, but I usually cut them for bouquets and settle for admiring the sturdy sword-shaped leaves for the rest of the season.

I've had botrytis hit this plant (botrytis crown rot leaves the rhizomes in such a mushy state it's truly disgusting). I whacked it out, replanted a bit of the rhizome at the normal level and had it come back within a very short time. Grows to 4 feet (120 cm).

I. ensata (syn. *I. kaempferi*) in the nursery trade is the Japanese iris. One of the most glamorous and elegant of all the irises, it has large, flat blossoms. They bloom in June in intense blues, purples, pink, whites, reds and bicolors. They include single, double, triple, multi-petalled and more forms. Grows to 3 feet (90 cm). Through years and years of selection, some really glorious varieties have been developed. They need a wet site that's well drained in winter.

Irises can be in a patch on their own because the foliage is so wonderful in all three seasons. But they work well with an enormous variety of other

PLANTING & MAINTENANCE TIPS

❦ The roots of *I. ensata* and *I. sibirica* are stringy and they like moist, slightly acid soil (a pH between 5.5 and 6.5) and plenty of humus. Plant crowns 2" – 3" (5 cm – 7.5 cm) deep and about 1½ feet (45 cm) apart in early fall or spring. Always give them a protected site.

❦ Irises don't need mulching, and it might cause fungus.

❦ Add a little bone meal around the plants but not fertilizers high in nitrogen, which promotes rapid soft growth.

❦ When dividing, make sure you take a large enough chunk. They tend to regenerate slowly.

General iris care:

❦ Sun, good drainage and good soil are the primary cultural requirements.

❦ Plant in midsummer; set the rhizomes so they are just barely covered with soil. Stir up the soil around them.

❦ Divide after flowering; keep the fans turned outward.

❦ Bearded irises must have at least six hours of sun a day and well-drained soil on the limy side. Persistent wet will make them croak.

❦ When plants go dormant after June, they won't need watering until the fall, but water before the soil gets too cold.

❦ Hand weed so as not to disturb root systems.

❦ They don't like competition, which explains why you so often see iris beds set out on their own.

perennials. Let them take over from narcissus as they pass on to ruined glory. Certainly put them near peonies. And grow small ground covers such as *Viola labradorica* or one of the tradescantias (spiderwort) or *Hemerocallis*, daylily, with them. Use them along edges of a country garden, near water at the cottage, by a pond, or near ornamental grasses.

OTHER SPECIES & CULTIVARS

Here is a short list of iris types.

Non-bulbous, or rhizomatous, irises:
All of these are divided into sections and more subsections and series.

1. Broad-leaved, rhizomed, bearded (pogon) types such as *I. x germanica*. These are commonly called flags. The beard is made of hairs that supposedly help bees on their fertilization trips into the flower. Usually sold in the fall. At least from mail-order sources.

2. Narrow-leaved, thick rhizomes or beardless (apogon) types—these are the Siberian or grass irises such as *I. sibirica*. Siberian irises are very hardy and have fibrous roots and reed-like elegant leaves. They prefer moist soil that doesn't dry out. Add peat, compost and manure to top dress. Grows to 4 feet (120 cm). Because they take some shade, you can plant them with hostas.

3. Slender rhizomed crested types such as *I. cristata* are native to eastern North America. This tiny woodland plant grows to 10 inches (25 cm) and has sword-shaped leaves.

Bulbous irises:

I. histrioides is pale blue; *I. danfordiae* is a bright yellow that blooms early in spring—in fact, the smaller the iris, the earlier it seems to bloom. *I. reticulata* is purple and blue. Foliage for these bulbs must be allowed to ripen, so plant with later-blooming perennials to cover them up.

I. pumila, Dwarf Iris are early spring flowering. These are tiny replicas of the Tall Bearded Iris and come in all colors. Their early spring appearance is reassuring that all's well with the garden. Heights vary from 6 inches (15 cm) to 12 inches (30 cm). Taller yet are the Lilliput hybrids to 18 inches (45 cm). Rowancroft Yellow is an intermediate Tall Bearded and early June flowering and a good companion to B.Y. Morrison the earliest flowering of the Iris germanica (Tall Bearded Iris) with blue flowers.

Lysimachia clethroides

FAMILY NAME: *Primulaceae* / ZONE: 3
PHOTOGRAPHED IN: University of British Columbia Botanical Gardens

There are few plants that I think of in wholly anthropomorphic terms, but *Lysimachia clethroides* is one of them. A humorous plant—it doesn't look peculiar, but a sense of humor seems part of its structure. It's commonly called the gooseneck loosestrife, and indeed in a small drift it looks as though it's part of a gaggle of geese.

That these plants are called loosestrife is confusing. The purple loosestrife that haunts the wetlands of North America, scooping up habitats as it spreads, is in a completely different family (*Lythraceae*) from this loosestrife. *Lythrum salicaria*, purple loosestrife, is incredibly invasive. The lysimachias from the primrose family are spreaders but won't invade the countryside.

Lysimachias creep, bolt, stand erect—do everything but climb. There are 165 to 200 species in the genus. *L. clethroides* came into my garden through a hortbuddy, and I thought the one little stalk he gave me with a few bits of root sticking out at the end looked a bit mingy. Little did I know. It turned into a perfectly glorious drift of white within a year or so,

Lysimachia clethroides

❧ Lysimachias will make do with just about any soil. But the richer and moister it is, the faster they'll spread. They grow in sun or shade.

❧ There is absolutely no problem about propagating these plants. I've jerked a chunk out of the ground, put it in another spot and had it root within a few days. The creeping form needs only a stone or some soil on a part of one of the trailing shoots to root. Each new rooting section will cover 3 square feet (0.3 square metres) so be warned—this fulfills all definitions of a super ground cover, invasive being the main one.

and now I hand out little chunks to forewarned friends.

It has dense white spiky flowers at the end of branchless stalks, and the racemes of flowers take a dip, giving them the goose-like look. I grow it with *Coreopsis verticillata* 'Moonbeam'; *Lobelia siphilitica*, great blue lobelia; and *Physostegia virginiana* 'Variegata', variegated obedient plant. They are all the same size, and the pink, yellow and blue in these plants are pure enough to work well with each other.

I very much like *L. nummularia*, creeping Jenny. It is a superb ground cover, since each rooted cutting will cover about 3 square feet (0.3 square metres). I've used it in places where a fast cover was needed to protect the soil from erosion. The leaves are bright green and the little yellow flowers brilliant in early summer. It grows beautifully in the shade and is easy to pull up once its mission is fulfilled. There is a golden form, with both leaves and flowers in a mellow, pale tone, though it is much slower; it's choice as a background plant to hostas and muscari.

OTHER SPECIES & CULTIVARS

L. ciliata looks like *L. punctata* but isn't as invasive.

L. nummularia, creeping Jenny, moneywort (I've also heard it called creeping Charlie, but I always think of a specific weed when I hear that name). This native of Europe has naturalized itself all over North America; a terrific container plant either by itself trailing all over the place or in with other golden plants.

'Aurea' will add touches of gold wherever it is planted.

L. punctata, yellow loosestrife, is rather coarser than the other loosestrifes; a native of Europe, it too has naturalized all over the place, especially in ditches. It's a hardworking plant and will sit in a damp, darkish place and continue to bloom for weeks on end. A good plant for the country or wild garden, where it can ramp about at will.

Nepeta x *faassenii*
'Dropmore Blue'

FAMILY NAME: *Labiatae* / ZONE: 4
PHOTOGRAPHED IN: Park & Tilford Gardens, North Vancouver

Nepeta x *faassenii* 'Dropmore Blue'

Many gardeners spend a lot of time looking for blue plants. One garden I particularly like has edging down one side of a raised bed that alternates *Nepeta* x *faassenii* 'Dropmore Blue' and *Stachys byzantina*, lamb's-ears. The blue and silver combination is a show stopper.

Nepeta, or catmints, aren't to be confused with catnip. That's *Nepeta cataria*. I've noticed, however, that a lot of cats (including my own) aren't aware that catmint isn't the stuff they're supposed to get high on. They chew away and roll around on it anyway. Eventually they get bored with this exercise and leave the plant alone. In spite of this treatment, it thrives, and the soft gray foliage and bright blue flowers give enormous pleasure.

This is such a frankly old-fashioned plant that an old-fashioned border looks a little empty without it. Even if they get some winterkill, they will come back, sometimes a little slowly, from the base in spring.

Nepetas can form low-growing hedges because the stiff foliage is easy to keep pruned to shape. It's perfect for the herb garden, where it should be allowed to grow as large as possible.

There is some confusion between the most famous of all the hybrids: *N. x faassenii* is the most readily available. Its parents are *N. mussinii* and *N. nepetella*. Often it gets labelled *N. mussinii*, so you might be buying the same thing if you purchase both. See below for the difference in these two plants.

N. x faassenii is the best plant for the June garden, and the lavender blue flowers bloom into fall. Each time you touch the plant it releases some of its fragrance from the aromatic leaves. The silver-gray leaves and blue flowers growing up the stem make a good vertical line. Grows to 2 feet (60 cm) high and about 18 inches (45 cm) wide in a vigorous clump. It's sterile, so you don't have to worry about it scattering seeds around.

'Dropmore Blue' is a hybrid form that I think is the best of all. It has lavender blue flowers with the usual silver-gray ethereal foliage.

PLANTING & MAINTENANCE TIPS

❧ Plant in the sun. However, I have some in part shade and they grow well enough, though with a tendency to flop over more than those that grow in full sun.

❧ Nepetas are hardy in all but the coldest regions. They are drought resistant— that is, if they get somewhat dried out on occasion they will continue to live. Needs well-drained soil. Like many aromatic herbs, they come from areas where the soil is poor and thin and rainfall is varied. Too rich a soil and they tend to get awkward and leggy.

❧ Divide in spring where the weather is cold, before it blooms.

❧ Sow seeds in April to May where the weather permits.

❧ Clip back after the first bloom and usually (not always) they come back with a second, though less prolific, bloom. Don't cut back in fall—most of these plants do much better when they are left alone as winter protection.

❧ If frost kills foliage, usually it will come back from the roots or base in the spring.

❧ Most pests (except cats) leave these plants alone.

Nepeta x *faassenii* 'Dropmore Blue'

OTHER SPECIES & CULTIVARS

N. cataria, catnip, is not a great garden plant, but bees as well as cats love it. If you do grow it, put it where cats can have it off in private and where they won't be disturbing other plants. Grows to 3 feet (1 m).

N. mussinii is more floppy than *N.* x *faassenii*, the foliage grayer, hairier and broader. This native of the Caucasus Mountains has blue flowers and seeds itself with great abandon. Grows to 1 foot (30 cm); zone 3.

'Blue Wonder' blooms June to July in sun or part shade. Grows to 18 inches (45 cm).

'Snowflake' is a white form.

N. nervosa, native of Kashmir, has green-veined leaves with cylindrical spikes of bright blue or yellow flowers. Grows to 2 feet (60 cm).

N. sibirica, native of Siberia, an indication of its hardiness, has lance-shaped leaves with tiny hairs on the underside. The flowers are more on the purple-blue side and seem to go on all summer. I have it with lilies and phlox—a great combination. Zone 3.

'Blue Beauty', zone 3, and x 'Souvenir d'André Chaudon' are more invasive than any of the other forms.

Paeonia

FAMILY NAME: *Ranunculacae* / ZONE: 4 to 8
PHOTOGRAPHED IN THE GARDENS OF: Kathy Leishman and Don and Helen Nesbitt

A h, peonies! Much beloved by artists who see a whole world of sensuality in their magnificent faces, peonies bloom for a few glorious weeks, and even if you are clever and work out a system of having early to late-season peonies, it will still last only six weeks in all. But it doesn't matter—these plants have foliage that is attractive all summer. They turn gold or bronze-red in the fall and then fade away into the ground for the winter. There are herbaceous peonies that die right to the ground in winter, and tree peonies that have a woody base. All peonies bloom in late spring or early summer.

Peonies have tuberous roots and large, sumptuous leaves that are amiable with almost all the other plants that come along after them. They grow to just over 3 feet (1 m) high and are about the same width, making them a good prop for other plants. Most of the old-fashioned ones need

Paeonia

❧ The farther north you garden, the more sun peonies will take. In hot areas, give them a bit of shade. The most important part of peony culture is to plant in the fall (September to hard frost) and make sure they have a large enough space both for planting and for site. Dig out a hole a couple of feet (60 cm) wide and the same depth. If this seems large, it will pay off with a long-lived healthy plant. Add a fair amount of compost and manure to it. Make sure the peony tubers aren't planted too deep. The buds, or eyes, should be no deeper than 2 inches (5 cm) below the surface, even shallower in warm areas. If they are too deep, the plant won't bloom.

❧ Water very deeply in spring and again in fall to make sure the roots are well fed. Drainage should be good as well—they don't like wet feet.

❧ Clean rotting foliage up immediately and add to the compost heap.

❧ Leave peonies alone for at least 12 years. Then they can be divided in autumn. Make sure there are three eyes on each piece.

❧ Botrytis is a major problem showing up as rot and is usually brought on by long wet spells or overwatering. Remove the blighted pieces and get rid of them.

some kind of staking because the big blowsy blooms tend to flop over the minute rain touches them.

The showy flowers come in a wide range of colors, from a rich ruby red through to the palest of pale pinks and white. The pale ones are especially fragrant. If you have a peony that refuses to bloom, it might be planted too deeply (see Planting & Maintenance Tips).

I inherited several of the huge, old-fashioned kind, which seem to bloom for about ten minutes. One great pleasures is to cut them just before the bloom fully opens and hang them upside down to dry for a couple of weeks. In a dried arrangement they look like magnificent ancient silk flowers.

I prefer the simpler single-petalled forms. A favorite is a cultivar called 'Cheddar Gold', which has a row of white petals around rich gold stamens.

One grouping I enjoy very much is peonies with fall-blooming plants such as *Anemone* x *hybrida* 'September Charm' or 'Honorine Jobert' with *Alchemilla mollis* around their feet.

Peonies are the best cover-up for spring bulbs, especially narcissus. But these mustn't be planted too close—it might harm the tubers. Put little bulbs such as alliums and scillas at least 8 inches (20 cm) away from the extreme edges of the tubers, and anything larger at least 1 foot (30 cm) away. Peonies are also a superb background for Siberian irises and lower-growing hardy geraniums.

Paeonia

OTHER SPECIES & CULTIVARS

P. lactiflora (syn. *P. albiflora* or *P. sinensis*) is from China. Semi-double and fully double blooms in red, pink and white in 100 distinct varieties. The parent of most of the hybrids we see now. They grow to 3 ½ feet (1 m). Here are some of the better-known ones:

Doubles: 'Alice Harding', light pink; 'Festiva Maxima', with white blooms and crimson flecks in the centre; 'Kansas', bright red; 'Mrs. Franklin Roosevelt', pale pink.

Single or semi-doubles: 'Argosy'; 'Tree Peony'; 'Silver Sails'.

P. mlokokosewitschii, commonly called Molly the Witch, is early blooming; has gray leaves and yellow flowers.

P. officinalis, native of Europe, is another old species, mainly used in medicine, or at least in mythology, as a curative. Grows to 3 ½ feet (1 m) and has several varieties.
   'Alba Plena', double white; 'Rubra Plena', double crimson. 'Rosea Plena', double pink.

P. suffruticosa, tree peony, native to western China, has been in cultivation for about 1,500 years. Tree peonies are May blooming, woody plants in single and semi-double forms with rose pink to white flowers. In the right site they can grow to 7 feet (1.5 m) and the same width. Cultivars range in color from pale yellow, golds and apricot into deep reds and purples.

P. tenuifolia, native to the Caucasus Mountains, is the species that contains the fringed peony, with finely divided, almost fennel-like, foliage. Flowers are crimson with yellow stamens. This smaller variety grows to 1 foot (30 cm). Disappears by midsummer; has quite brittle roots and is not easy to move. This is the earliest flowering peony.

Phlox paniculata 'Mount Fujiyama'

FAMILY NAME: *Polemoniaceae* / ZONE: 4
PHOTOGRAPHED IN: University of British Columbia Botanical Gardens

I t's impossible not to love these plants. Any garden would be seriously lacking without them. They come along and bloom with reckless abandon just about the time everything else in the spring garden has decided to pack it in. This is especially true of *Phlox paniculata*, the perfect plant to create a bridge from spring into summer.

Native to North America, they come in just about every size and for every light condition possible. There are phloxes that do well in woodland gardens, others for a meadow, yet others for the rock garden; there are dwarfs and giants.

The opposite leaves are lobed or notched, and the flowers are large crowded clusters at the end of long stems. They are fragrant, though very subtly so—this is not a major hit of scent.

Phlox are divided into three groups, depending on the culture, or growing needs, of each species:

Woodland species: *P. divaricata* and *P. stolonifera* require moist, humus-rich soil. They thrive in light to full shade and form evergreen carpets of foliage that almost never need dividing. They add rich color to a shade or native wildflower garden. Interplant with spring bulbs, near ferns and hostas and other ground covers, such as tiarellas.

PLANTING & MAINTENANCE TIPS

❧ The soil requirements of the three groups of phloxes are noted in the listing. Water in hot weather. Divide every three or four years—in spring in cold regions, in fall in warmer regions. They must have good air circulation.

❧ As soon as the flowers start looking ratty or brown, I cut them back to the nearest node below. If they seed themselves about, the issue is a rather dull, vaguely lavender color.

❧ Be sure to mulch in both spring and fall with compost and manure.

Cushion or low-mounding phlox: *P. bifida, P. douglasii, P. subulata* and *P.* x 'Chattahoochee'. These require ordinary to lean well-drained soil in full sun; ideal in the rock garden or to soften hard edges of stone paths. They will take over from the early spring flowering of *Arabis caucasica.*

Border phlox: *P. carolina, P. maculata, P. paniculata.* All require rich, moist but well-drained soil. They can take both full sun and high light shade. They do best in cool summers. In areas of high humidity, they succumb to powdery mildew. I can't resist these plants, so I spray them with a fungicide in spring (see "General Plant Care" in the Introduction), and if they habitually develop mildew I move them to more open spaces. Look for resistant cultivars.

Border phloxes can be placed almost anywhere successfully as long as they have breathing room for the spread. I have them combined with filipendulas, hardy geraniums and astilbes.

Phlox paniculata is purple in the species, but the cultivated varieties (cultivars) are wide ranging: violet, pink, white and red. They have five-petalled tubular flowers and look a little like primroses crowded at the end of the leafy stalks. *P. p.* 'Mount Fujiyama' is my favorite. The white of the spires is so pure, and it flowers later than almost all the other phloxes and blooms all September.

I don't like to see the tall phloxes all by themselves. They look much better mixed in with other plants to disguise the not terribly elegant stalks. They don't need much care. Keep them deadheaded, and cut any weak stalks right back to the ground.

OTHER SPECIES & CULTIVARS

P. bifida, prairie phlox; flowers range from white to soft blue with deeply cleft petals; a cushion type. Add to your supply by taking basal cuttings in fall. Cultivate in sandy soil in full sun. Grows to 10 inches (25 cm).

P. carolina (syn. *P. suffruticosa*) 'Miss Lingard' is a favorite—it has white flowers and blooms for weeks through June and July. I've never had a problem with mildew on this one. Grows 3 feet (1 m); zone 3.

P. divaricata, wild blue phlox, has light lavender blue flowers; semi-evergreen ground cover; spreads 1 foot (30 cm).

P. maculata, wild sweet William, pink to purple flowers bloom throughout summer. Grows to 3 feet (1 m); zone 3.

P. paniculata, common garden phlox, has such a huge variety of cultivars you don't need to settle for the rather dull-looking magenta one that looks like lingerie silk. Here are a few: 'Blue Boy' is a nice clear blue; 'Bright Eyes' has a red eye in pink blossoms; 'Starfire', a brilliant magenta that's difficult to place with other plants but worth a try with anything white; 'Rembrandt' and 'White Admiral' have white flowers.

P. stolonifera, creeping phlox, native to the eastern United States, has purple-violet flowers that bloom in April and May; zones 2 to 3.

P. subulata, moss pink, is everywhere, but it's such a charmer I wouldn't do without it in the garden. 'Blue Emerald', 'May Snow', 'Pink Emerald', 'White Delight'.

Phlox paniculata
'Mount Fujiyama'

Ruta graveolens 'Jackman's Blue'

FAMILY NAME: *Rutaceae* / ZONE: 5
PHOTOGRAPHED IN THE GARDEN OF: Pamela Frost

Ruta graveolens 'Jackman's Blue'

This genus is a small part of the family *Rutaceae*, which includes more than 600 shrubs and trees. The most famous of its relatives are citruses and *Choisya*, Mexican orange blossom bush. There are 40 to 60 species that come from the Mediterranean and western Asia, but only one that's widely used in domestic gardens.

Rues have been honored since Greek and Roman times as a curative for poisons and as an antidote for spells. Supposedly, it kills fleas. It certainly has a pungent odor, and some people may get skin rashes from handling this plant on very warm sunny days when the scent is released.

R. graveolens, common rue, is native to the Mediterranean, where it grows on dry rocky soil. The foliage is deeply notched, and some of the hybrid forms are almost blue. Leafy flower stalks are topped by flattened branched clusters of small acid yellow flowers, which are rather dull. Grows from a woody base where the leaves have longer stalks than those higher up. It has a long branched tap root. In general, they grow 2' – 3' (60 cm – 1 m) high and the same width.

R. g. 'Jackman's Blue' is a cultivar with stunning steely blue, almost wavy foliage and acid yellow-green flowers. A compact plant; grows to 2 feet (60 cm). 'Curly Girl', another handsome hybrid that I like, has ruffled edges to the blue leaves.

Rues have many functions in the garden. They make a forceful contrast to a felted gray annual such as *Helichrysum petiolatum* and an *Acer palmatum* 'Dissectum Atropurpureum' that has even more deeply cut foliage than the rue. Use them as an adjunct to a fine foliage plant such as *Santolina chamaecyparissus*—they can both be clipped for shape and are amazingly good with each other. *Alchemilla mollis*, Lady's-mantle, is a natural companion for rues.

As a low formal hedge for a border this is an ideal plant. It responds well to pruning, or it can be left alone as a specimen in a herb garden. Combine it with *Lavandula angustifolia*, English lavender, and *Hyssopus officinalis*, hyssop, for an aromatic group with wonderful contrasts in foliage textures and colors. Rues can be used in small knot gardens, since they root readily from cuttings.

The caterpillars of Monarch butterflies are attracted to this plant and will strip it of leaves pretty easily. If you are in the migratory path of this glorious butterfly, you might want to consider planting it as an aid to the butterflies.

OTHER SPECIES & CULTIVARS

R. graveolens 'Variegata' has cream and white edges and splotches on the foliage. Best pruned regularly. Grows to 1½ feet (45 cm); zone 4.

Salvia x 'Superba'

FAMILY NAME: *Labiatae* / ZONE: 4; 3 to 9 depending on variety
PHOTOGRAPHED IN: VanDusen Botanical Garden

I n the garden of exquisite taste, salvias have a bad reputation, based on the eyeball-searing annual salvias so beloved of bedding-out gardeners. But there are salvias and there are salvias. The perennial salvias, the sages, are extremely important plants. They range from mounded to an almost subshrub size with tubular flowers and have the usual square stems typical of any genus in the *Labiatae* family. There are hundreds—as many as 750—of species, but only a few that we use or can even get in nurseries. They generally come from the Mediterranean and Asia.

The foliage is aromatic and the leaves are either oval or lance-shaped. They have fibrous roots and woody crowns. It's hard to find a plant that salvias don't look good with: yarrows, sedums, coneflowers, coreopsis or ornamental grasses. If you can't find the more interesting forms of salvias, join societies to get seeds. Salvias don't need staking, most are drought resistant, and pests leave them alone. And they are related to the cooking herb.

S. officinalis is our traditional sage that is good not only in cooking but

PLANTING & MAINTENANCE TIPS

❧ This is a tolerant, easy-to-grow plant. It likes rich, fertile soil that's fairly moist but well drained. Though it will take a little shade, this plant really needs lots of sun to do well. It will inevitably get much too leggy in shade. In the right conditions, it's fairly drought tolerant.

❧ Cut off the tops once there's been a killing frost. Mulch to at least 2 inches (5 cm) after the ground has frozen.

❧ Cut back to the ground in early spring.

❧ Divide in early fall or spring every three or four years. Add lots of organic matter to the soil every year.

❧ Few pests bother this plant, except whitefly and spider mites.

Salvia x 'Superba'

also in the garden. I've always thought it was unkillable, but that isn't true. A particularly bad winter sitting around with feet locked in ice managed to make a 10-year-old plant croak. The blue-green foliage is aromatic and very attractive. It has little blue insignificant flowers. I grow it with hyssop, another fragrant herb, with bright blue flowers, and they look just right together.

Salvias make almost any combination a more romantic group. I like them with stachys and lavenders and, of course, with the sage-scented perovskias. Any plant with pink or blue blossoms such as chrysanthemums, delphiniums or hardy geraniums will work well with salvias.

S. x *superba* (syn. *S. virgata*, *S. nemorosa* and *S. virgata nemorosa*) is sold under many names, as indicated in brackets. You'll have to sort that one out with your nurseryperson.

OTHER SPECIES & CULTIVARS

S. argentea, silver sage, is a stunning silver felted or hairy low plant. Put in pots and move around to keep it in the hottest part of the garden. Grows 6" – 8" (15 cm – 20 cm). Biennial habit.

S. azurea var. *grandiflora* (syn. *S. pitcheri*) has long racemes of sky blue flowers. It will sprawl all over the place if it's allowed; stake it, or plant it next to a tall plant to lean on; or cut back in July to cramp the growth. Will grow to 4 feet (1.2 m). Hardy to zone 5 and colder regions if there's reliable snow cover.

S. guaranitica, brilliant blue but dark blooms; survives winter in zone 8.

S. officinalis, common sage, is the herb that you use in poultry stuffing. In addition to its usefulness, it is a glorious small shrubby plant with silver to gray foliage.

'Purpurascens' is a more purply form of sage; not hardy even in zone 6, but looks so splendid it's worth a try even if you use it only as an annual. In a really protected spot, with 4 inches (10 cm) of mulching, it might make it through the winter, but will probably suffer from die-back. In that case, cut it back to any new growth and hope for a fresh spurt.

'Tricolor'; this curious plant is purple, green and cream. Not all that easy to place, but try it in a pot.

S. patens, gentian sage, is a pure blue; can take very little frost; treat it as an annual if you live in an area colder than zone 8.

S. pratensis (syn. *S. haematodes*), meadow sage, lavender blue flowers; basal foliage. Zone 3.

S. sclarea, clary sage, has mauve flowers and dark, wrinkled leaves; grows to 4 feet (1.2 m). Biennial.

S. x *superba*; violet-blue flowering spikes bloom for three to four weeks in early to midsummer. The leaves are typical of most salvias—wrinkled and soft with a toothy, rounded shape. The lower ones are mostly stalkless. The gray-green leaves are described as sage green, of course. The base is woody. Grows to $3\frac{1}{2}$ feet (90 cm).

'Blue Queen' has violet flowers; grows to 2 feet (60 cm) high.

'East Friesland' is deep purple; compact growth to $1\frac{1}{2}$ feet (45 cm); zones 4 to 7.

'Rose Queen' has rosy violet flowers; grows to 2 feet (60 cm). All zone 4.

Scabiosa *caucasica*

FAMILY NAME: *Dipsacaceae* / ZONE: 2 to 3
PHOTOGRAPHED IN: University of British Columbia Botanical Gardens

W hy a plant with such a sensuous face and gentle appearance has a
dreadful name like *Scabiosa* lies in horticultural history. Alas, poor
Scabiosa got its name because in medieval times it was grown by herbalists
to cure scabies, a dreaded affliction of the time. It comes from the Latin
scabies, the itch.

   Scabiosa caucasica is one of the hardiest perennials for late summer. It
blooms from June to September and is a great cutting plant. Rosettes of

Scabiosa caucasica

mauve flowers with yellow centres perch on the end of leafless, slightly hairy stems; leaves are smooth and gray-green. This perennial is short–lived where summers are hot and dry even though it is from hot countries.

There are from 60 to 100 species, from mostly Mediterranean regions. If you haven't had a lot of experience growing perennials from seed, this is a good one to start with.

I prefer this plant mixed in with others rather than as a drift on its own. It's a fine companion for sun lovers such as Asiatic lilies.

I hide the long bare stems with lower, more fleshy plants such as *Lychnis coronaria*, which has incredible fuzzy gray foliage and magenta flowers. This may be too much for some gardeners, and it's certainly startling in my own garden, which tends to be quiet. A slightly more subtle group is scabiosa with *Iberis sempervirens*, perennial candytuft. It has low, dense foliage and bright white flowers.

PLANTING & MAINTENANCE TIPS

❧ Scabiosas thrive in slightly alkaline soil with a sunny exposure. Full sun is absolutely necessary. They don't like wet feet in winter, which is why I've had to move mine to a fairly high well-drained area.

❧ Divide almost any time from August to the end of September every two to four years.

❧ Top dress with plenty of compost or well-rotted manure or an organic fertilizer in spring, then again in summer. The colder the area, the thicker the mulch.

OTHER SPECIES & CULTIVARS

S. atropurpurea, native to southern Europe; deep crimson, fragrant pincushion-type flowers bloom all summer; deeply lobed leaves. Grows easily when planted in spring directly in place. Grows to 2 ½ feet (75 cm).

'Double Mixed' has purple, deep crimson or pink and white flowers; grows to 3 feet (1 m).

'Dwarf Double Mixed' grows to 18 inches (45 cm).

S. caucasica

'Clive Greaves' has large lavender blue flowers.

'Miss Willmott' is creamy white.

S. lucida has rosy lilac pincushion-type flowers all summer; grows to 8 inches (20 cm).

Sedum x 'Vera Jameson'

FAMILY NAME: *Crassulaceae* / ZONE: 3
PHOTOGRAPHED IN THE GARDEN OF: Pamela Frost

I once visited a magnificent garden in the south of France that had greenhouse after greenhouse of *Crassulaceae*. It seemed that no color or size was missed in the collection. I was much chastened—who could compare the little bit of collecting you can do in a small garden with something like that? But I did come away with even greater respect and love for sedums.

Drought tolerant, they provide winter interest, and in this genus alone there are from 300 to 600 species. They grow all over North America.

The thick fleshy leaves are the plant's strategy for handling drought: they fill with water and continue to feed the roots long after other plants have succumbed. As ground covers they are nonpareil, and many of the larger, more erect forms are absolute musts in the mixed border. These plants are an excellent source of new material. You've only to break off a stalk and stick it in the ground and it will begin to develop roots.

Generally speaking, the leaves develop in overlapping spirals, either

Sedum alboroseum
'Medio-variegatum'

alternate or sometimes opposite. If you have a really difficult site, such as rocky, poor soil tending to drain quickly, sedums would be good plants.

S. × 'Vera Jameson' is a sedum I found only a few years ago. It has all the typical elements of sedums: fleshy stalks, good ground covering, pretty late-summer flowers. But the flesh is a deep purple-gray, the edging a marvel of deeper purple, and bright pink flowers emerge in late summer. Grows to only 9" – 12" (22 cm – 30 cm), with a spread of 1 foot (30 cm), but is so striking that it needs a place where it can be seen easily.

I have a 'Vera Jameson' near *Euphorbia myrsinites,* which has gray fleshy leaves, and *Artemisia* 'Powis Castle', with its fine silky threadlike foliage. This is a marvellous container plant when placed so you can see the interesting foliage. Or grow it at the front of the border.

Sedums for rock gardens—there are some incredibly dwarf forms, real little beauties the collecting gardener should look out for.

OTHER SPECIES & CULTIVARS

S. × 'Autumn Joy'; parents are *S. spectabile* and *S. telephium,* so you may find either identification on plant labels in nurseries. It makes a pleasing clump that always stays erect, with gray-green stems and flat-topped heads that turn into a mass of star-like flowers as the summer wears on. The pink flowers turn to brick red as autumn moves

Sedum × 'Vera Jameson'

❧ Sedums grow in almost any good soil with really good drainage. Never over-water. If they get too much (such as during a moist summer), they may develop fungal diseases or root rot. Let the soil dry out almost completely before water-ing. They don't need fertilizing—especially not nitrogen, which makes the stems flop over. They need full sun, though I have some of the low-growing species in areas with a bit of shade.

❧ These are incredibly easy to propagate. In the case of the larger, more erect types, break off a piece of the stalk at a joint, stick it into the ground and it will start grow-ing a new plant. With the ground-covering ones, even a small section will root.

❧ Except for the possibility of fungal disease from overwatering, nothing much bothers these plants.

in; don't cut them back in fall and you'll make a pleasant mound for winter. Grows to 2 feet (60 cm).

S. acre, gold moss, golden carpet, is ubiquitous because it is so easy to make a compact covering in even the poorest soil. The foliage is minute fleshy spikes with bright yellow flowers. Sun to partial shade. Good in pots.

S. kamtschaticum has yellow flowers on unbranched stems with glossy dark green toothed leaves that grow the whole length of the stem and turn dark red in autumn. Grows to 6 inches (15 cm) with a spread of 1 foot (30 cm).

'Variegatum' has creamy edges and grows more slowly. Grows to 1 foot (30 cm); needs sun. Zone 3.

S. middenendorffianum, very like the above, and often listed as a subspecies, but small-er and more finely structured. Yellow flowers bloom in late summer; lance-shaped bronze leaves; zone 3.

S. sieboldii has bright pink flowers in fall; round blue-green leaves edged in pink. The arching stems grow to 4 inches (10 cm). Zone 4.

S. spathulifolium; this native of the West Coast, from British Columbia to California, is a great little plant with yellow flowers and leaves that are gray rosettes and become greener in the shade. Grows 2 inches (5 cm) high. Zone 4.

S. spectabile, native of China and Korea; herbaceous; gray-green leaves with flat-topped rosy pink flowers at the end of the stalks. Grows to 2 feet (60 cm).

'Variegatum' has subtle pale yellow variegation.

S. spurium has deep pink flowers in autumn followed by bright red foliage. A good ground cover. It will root wherever the stems have ground contact. Sprawls about on 6 inch (15 cm) stems. Needs sun. Zone 3.

'Dragon's Blood' has dark red leaves in spring that eventually turn green.

Stachys byzantina

FAMILY NAME: *Labiatae* / ZONE: 4
PHOTOGRAPHED IN: University of British Columbia Botanical Gardens

S omeone once remarked about my garden, "You sure seem to like *Stachys*." I was a little surprised because I hadn't noticed how much I had allowed it to grow.

There are more than 300 species of this herbaceous perennial, and just three of them are in the nursery trade. Like all the other species in this family, they have square stems.

S. byzantina (syn. *S. lanata*, *S. olympica*) spreads easily but slowly on soft, hairy almost silver-white stems. I haven't met a kid yet who wasn't fascinated stroking the velvety long leaves and stems. The flowers are a rather uninteresting lavender pink. Grows 9" – 18" (22 cm – 45 cm) tall.

As an edging plant, *Stachys* is perfect. It's also a wonderful carpeting plant because it creeps along and makes a dense silver mat. It is immensely hardy, and about the only thing it won't stand up to is wet soil, in which it will rot.

My favorite gardens all have this plant at the front of the border backed by hardy geraniums, peonies and thalictrum. It provides strong contrasts in both texture and colors. If you have grass growing to the edges of your perennial borders, this plant will certainly make a good definition for them.

I have it as an edger to what I consider my cutting garden. This area is filled with all the tulips I've taken from other parts of the garden. As they fade away, the stachys takes off and covers up any dying foliage. Combines well with more open plants such as *Sisyrinchium*, blue-eyed grass, with bright blue flowers backed by *Coreopsis verticillata* 'Zagreb'.

PLANTING & MAINTENANCE TIPS

❧ Will take any well-drained soil, either sandy or loamy, in full sun up to part shade. Will succumb to rot if there is a particularly wet or humid summer, which explains the need for excellent drainage. Remove any shrivelled leaves immediately, since decaying leaves attract pests.

❧ If rot sets in, cut the plant right back. It will start regrowing.

Stachys byzantina

OTHER SPECIES & CULTIVARS

S. byzantina 'Silver Carpet' is a sterile cultivar with silvery leaves that doesn't produce flower spikes. An attractive plant that grows to 6 inches (15 cm) tall.

'Primrose Heron' has magenta blooms; yellow foliage in spring turns gray-green in summer.

S. grandiflora, betony, has pink to deep purple flowers; distinctive triangular green basal leaves with leafy upright stalks. Grows to 1½ feet (45 cm). Zone 2.

'Alba' has white flowers.

'Rosea' has deep rose pink flowers.

S. officinalis, wood betony, is similar to the above but has denser clusters of smaller, usually purple, flowers; zone 4.

Veronica *longifolia* 'Blauriesen'

FAMILY NAME: *Scrophulariaceae* / ZONE: 3
PHOTOGRAPHED IN: University of British Columbia Botanical Gardens

Veronicas glow with a radiance equalled by few other blooms of summer. The opulent color of its flowers and the deep green of the foliage make it a rich addition to the summer garden. The elegant graceful spires have rich blue blossoms and a fairly long flowering period in July.

There are two types: the spiky ones, and the trailing types with clusters of flowers at the end of each stem. They grow from woody crowns. The trailing types have smaller spikes and narrow, lance-shaped leaves.

Veronica longifolia 'Blauriesen'

V. longifolia is native in Europe and Asia. This clump-forming plant has ovate leaves and a stiff upright stalk about 1 foot (30 cm) long ending in spikes of lilac blue. It grows 2' – 4' (60 cm – 1.2 m), with a spread of 1 foot (30 cm). There are many cultivars, with 'Blauriesen' a particularly intense purple blue. 'Alba' is white.

There are plenty of weedy species of *Veronica* that will be familiar to anyone who enjoys wildflowers. *V. americana* sprawls about in wet places; *V. serpyllifolia* has creeping, sticky stems with short tubed flowers. *V. officinalis*, with hairy stems, is the plant that herbalists use in teas as a diuretic or in lotions for skin irritations. It grows in stony sites and clearings in woods.

Use dwarf forms in the rock garden; if you have poor soil, they'll do very well. There are some real beauties, and it's great to be able to look down on them with their midget spikes.

Veronica latifolia 'Crater Lake Blue' blooms magnificently with one of the best of all cut flowers, *Allium tuberosum*, garlic chives. Veronicas look good with other plants that have a rounded habit, such as *Achillea*, yarrow, and *Coreopsis*, tickseed. The ferny foliage of the former and the more airy open form of the latter make a splendid contrast to the thicker leaves of the veronica.

OTHER SPECIES & CULTIVARS

V. alpina is low and shrubby, with dark green leaves and small blue flowers at the end of the erect tips. A sprawler, it grows to 6 inches (15 cm).

V. gentianoides; the leaves are like gentian; needs richer soil than most rock garden plants. Forms mats with pale blue spikes. Grows to 18 inches (45 cm).

V. incana has lavender blue flowers and silver basal leaves; to 18 inches (45 cm).

V. prostrata has deep blue flowers, with gray hairy stems; mat-forming spreader; grows to 8 inches (25 cm).

V. spicata has blue or pink flowers and lance-shaped leaves; grows to 2 feet (60 cm), with a spread of 18 inches (45 cm). 'Nana' is a dwarf rock garden version; lavender blue flowers; grows to 6 inches (15 cm).

Bibliography

Bloom, Alan & Adrian. *Blooms of Bressingham Garden Plants.* London: HarperCollins, 1992.

Chatto, Beth. *The Dry Garden.* London: Dent, 1978.

Clausen, Ruth Rogers, and Nicolas H. Ekstrom. *Perennials for American Gardens.* New York: Random House, 1989.

Garland, Sarah. *The Herb Garden.* New York: Viking, 1984.

Harper, Pamela. *Designing with Perennials.* New York: Macmillan, 1991.

Harris, Marjorie. *The Canadian Gardener.* Toronto: Random House, 1990.

Hortus Third. New York: Macmillan, 1976.

McGourty, Frederick. *The Perennial Gardener.* Boston: Houghton Mifflin, 1989.

Magazines:

Canadian Gardening, Fine Gardening, Horticulture, National Gardening, Organic Gardening and *Plant & Garden.*

ZONE CHART		
Zone 1	below –50°F	(below –45°C)
Zone 2	–50 to –40°F	(–45 to –40°C)
Zone 3	–40 to –30°F	(–40 to –35°C)
Zone 4	–30 to –20°F	(–35 to –30°C)
Zone 5	–20 to –10°F	(–30 to –23°C)
Zone 6	–10 to 0°F	(–23 to –18°C)
Zone 7	0 to 10°F	(–18 to –12°C)
Zone 8	10 to 20°F	(–12 to –7°C)
Zone 9	20 to 30°F	(–7 to –1°C)
Zone 10	30 to 40°F	(–1 to 4°C)

Index